Come Home with Me!

Mary Elizabeth Salzmann

Consulting Editor Monica Marx, M.A./Reading Specialist

Published by SandCastle™, an imprint of ABDO Publishing Company, 4940 Viking Drive, Edina, Minnesota 55435.

Printed in the United States.

Credits
Edited by: Pam Price
Curriculum Coordinator: Nancy Tuminelly
Cover and Interior Design and Production: Mighty Media
Photo Credits: BananaStock, Ltd., Comstock, Corbis Images, Eyewire Images, PhotoDisc, Think Stock

Library of Congress Cataloging-in-Publication Data

Salzmann, Mary Elizabeth, 1968-
    Come home with me! / Mary Elizabeth Salzmann.
      p. cm. -- (Sight words)
    Includes index.
    Summary: Uses simple sentences, photographs, and a brief story to introduce six different words: as, how, if, new, then, with.
    ISBN 1-59197-465-8
    1. Readers (Primary) 2. Vocabulary--Juvenile literature. [1. Reading.] I. Title. II. Series.

PE1119.S2342155 2003
428.1--dc21

2003050314

SandCastle™ books are created by a professional team of educators, reading specialists, and content developers around five essential components that include phonemic awareness, phonics, vocabulary, text comprehension, and fluency. All books are written, reviewed, and leveled for guided reading, early intervention reading, and Accelerated Reader® programs and designed for use in shared, guided, and independent reading and writing activities to support a balanced approach to literacy instruction.

Let Us Know

After reading the book, SandCastle would like you to tell us your stories about reading. What is your favorite page? Was there something hard that you needed help with? Share the ups and downs of learning to read. We want to hear from you! To get posted on the ABDO Publishing Company Web site, send us e-mail at:

sandcastle@abdopub.com

SandCastle Level: Beginning

Featured Sight Words

as   how

if   new

then   with

Zach yells as he hits the ball.

How much can Jane and Ike eat?

Sam asks if he can help.

Faith has a new puppy.

Peg studies and then goes to bed.

Vic draws with a crayon.

Home Sweet Home

Pam and Will come home.

They sit in the family room with their parents.

They do their
homework as soon
as dinner is over.

Then, if there's time, they learn how to play a new game.

More Sight Words in This Book

a	in
and	is
can	much
come	the
do	their
eat	they
has	to
he	will

All words identified as sight words in this book are from Edward Bernard Fry's "First Hundred Instant Sight Words."

Picture Index

ball, p. 5

bed, p. 13

crayon, p. 15

dinner, p. 18

game, p. 20

puppy, p. 11

23

About SandCastle™

A professional team of educators, reading specialists, and content developers created the SandCastle™ series to support young readers as they develop reading skills and strategies and increase their general knowledge. The SandCastle™ series has four levels that correspond to early literacy development in young children. The levels are provided to help teachers and parents select the appropriate books for young readers.

Emerging Readers
(no flags)

Beginning Readers
(1 flag)

Transitional Readers
(2 flags)

Fluent Readers
(3 flags)

These levels are meant only as a guide. All levels are subject to change.

To see a complete list of SandCastle™ books and other nonfiction titles from ABDO Publishing Company, visit www.abdopub.com or contact us at:

4940 Viking Drive, Edina, Minnesota 55435 • 1-800-800-1312 • fax: 1-952-831-1632